ONE HUNDRED WAYS
TO A
Happy Bunny

ALSO BY CELIA HADDON IN THIS SERIES:

One Hundred Ways to a Happy Cat

One Hundred Ways to a Happy Dog

One Hundred Ways for a Cat
to Find Its Inner Kitten

One Hundred Ways for a Cat
to Train Its Human

One Hundred Ways to Live
With a Cat Addict

One Hundred Ways to Live
With a Dog Addict

One Hundred Ways to Friendship

One Hundred Ways to Say I Love You

One Hundred Ways to Serenity

One Hundred Kisses

ONE HUNDRED WAYS
TO A

Happy Bunny

BY
Celia Haddon

ILLUSTRATIONS BY
Jilly Wilkinson

HODDER &
STOUGHTON

Text copyright © 2007 by Celia Haddon
Illustrations copyright © 2007 by Jilly Wilkinson

First published in Great Britain in 2007

The right of Celia Haddon to be identified as the Author of
the Work has been asserted by her in accordance with the
Copyright, Designs and Patents Act 1988.

2

British Library Cataloguing in Publication Data
A record for this book is available from the British Library

ISBN-13: 978 0 340 909485
ISBN-10: 0340 90948X

Typeset in Baskerville by Avon DataSet Ltd,
Bidford-on-Avon, Warwickshire

Printed in the UK by CPI Bookmarque, Croydon, CR0 4TD

The paper and board used in this paperback are natural recyclable products
made from wood grown in sustainable forests. The manufacturing processes
conform to the environmental regulations of the country of origin.

Hodder & Stoughton
A Division of Hachette Children's Books
338 Euston Road
London NW1 3BH
www.madaboutbooks.com

This book is dedicated to Harvey, an inspirational house bunny, and to the memory of Happy, the house rabbit of my mother, Joyce Haddon, in the 1970s.

Contents

INTRODUCTION	9
BRINGING UP BABY	15
HOUSE AND GARDEN FOR BUNNIES	19
CARROT CUISINE	30
HOW CLEAN IS YOUR HUTCH?	41
HOME-SWEET-HOME BUNNY	46
FUN FOR BUN	58
SEX, LOVE AND FRIENDSHIP — BUNNY-STYLE	65
DOES AND DON'TS	75
A LONG AND HOPPY LIFE	80

USEFUL INFORMATION   90

ACKNOWLEDGEMENT   94

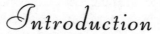

Introduction

A bunny is for life, not just for Easter. For twelve years, you will live with a loving, twitching nose, two long ears and a fluffy tail. Human loyalty and love are what makes a happy bunny.

A single bunny is a lonely bunny because rabbits are social animals. Try to make sure your bunny has a friend so that they can rabbit on together in their own language.

Your bunny's instinct is to be scared of anything new or strange. That's because his ancestors, the wild ones, were instant meals for foxes, dogs, cats and birds of prey. A wise rabbit watches out for danger and runs away. Understanding your bunny's timid nature will make you into his best human friend.

Bunnies don't make good pets for children under the age of ten. Rabbits don't like being cuddled or picked up and most children want a cuddly pet. Older children may grow out of them. A happy bunny needs a happy family.

Hop along to a rescue shelter rather than a pet shop. A good rescue shelter will introduce rabbits for you. They will also make sure you have the right accommodation for your new pet. Caring breeders don't sell their baby rabbits through pet shops. Your children will learn the joys of giving a rabbit a new life.

Buy the right breed. Giant breeds of rabbits need giant houses and giant runs, and cost more to feed. English lop rabbits have such long ears that they need extra large living space with no sharp edges, so that they don't hurt their own ears. Long-coated rabbits have bad hare days if they are not groomed every single day of their lives.

Don't keep a rabbit with a guinea pig. Neutered rabbits get on better together. Guinea pigs need different food and are in danger from rabbit bullying. How would you like to be housed with a chimpanzee or a gorilla?

Bunnies are most lively at dawn and dusk, so they make good pets for adults who work during the day – as long as they get plenty of attention, are not stuck in a hutch alone all day, and have a buddy bunny as a companion.

Bringing Up Baby

If you are getting baby rabbits, ask what breed and size they will be. You need to know how big the babies will grow so that you can buy (or make) a big enough house and run. If the seller doesn't know the answer, don't buy from them.

If you buy a bunny direct from a breeder, make sure the babies are used to living with humans. Baby rabbits should be handled by human beings daily between the ages of four and six weeks, or even

earlier, so that they become tame
pets. If this hasn't been done, they
may always be scared of humans.

Start socialising your baby
bunnies. Spend time with them.
Bring them small vegetable treats,
feed by hand, and develop the

human–rabbit bond. Handle her and pretend to groom her with a soft brush. Look at her nails so that she gets used to nail inspection. You want your baby to grow up into a Hugs Bunny. But remember babies need their quiet times too.

If they are going to be house rabbits, get them used to household noises like washing machines, doorbells, laughter, and music – anything from rock to Mozart. Some house bunnies enjoy watching TV!

Start gently training your bunny with tiny food rewards. Rabbits will respond to human words such as 'No', 'Stop', 'Come', 'Bedtime', and 'Into your box.' You can even clicker train them. Sometimes they know what you want them to do but still won't do it. Just like humans, really.

House and Garden for Bunnies

Think big when buying your rabbit's home. A hutch is not always the best home for a rabbit. Wendy houses, garden sheds, aviaries, summerhouses, dog kennels with runs, or even chicken houses can offer dream homes for rabbits. Bunnies deserve a stately home, not a hovel; after all they came over with the Normans, just like the English aristocracy!

If you do buy a hutch, get the biggest you can find. The minimum size for an average single rabbit is five feet long, two feet deep, and two feet high. Giant breeds or a pair of rabbits need much more space than that. The house must have a private sleeping compartment and a room for food bowls, hayrack, toys and a litter tray in the toilet area. Most of the hutches in a pet shop are too small and a 'starter' hutch is a no-hopper.

P ut the rabbit's outside hutch near the door you use most, so that you can visit it several times a day. A hutch at the bottom of the garden away from the house can mean a lonesome life of neglect for an unhappy rabbit.

R abbits love to do the bunny-
hop – to dance and leap
about. They can't do hareobics in a
rabbit hutch. There just isn't room.
So make sure you give them a large
run as well as a hutch. The
minimum size for a bunny garden
run is eight feet by four feet, and
two feet high. Remember that ark

runs are too low at the sides for your rabbit to sit there. Rabbits should have time in the run every day.

If the run is separate from the hutch, make sure it has a covered area to protect your bunny from rain and too much sun. Don't forget to supply clean water and some hay inside the run. Large builder's earthenware pipes provide shelter too.

You know you are a real rabbit-lover when you make your garden into a warren. If you are fencing the garden, remember to

keep cats, badgers and other predators out, as well as bunny in. Foxes, as well as bunnies, can dig under fencing.

Bunnies can even learn to use a cat flap if it is a light one. But make sure, if they come and go at will, that the garden is a safe area for them.

Ensure that your bunnies' stately home is completely weather-proof. Paint the outside with a pet-safe wood preservative. The roof should have a good overhang so that the water drips off away from the inside. Never paint or treat the inside because the chemicals will poison your bunnies if they start chewing the walls.

Location, location, location: make sure that your rabbit's home is sheltered from the wind, and from direct sun in summer. Move it indoors, into a shed or an unused garage in cold weather. A garage with cars in it is not safe because of fumes.

The best bedding is a deep layer of soft barley straw or good hay. Spread thick wood shavings (never sawdust) or rabbit litter in the latrine area. Whether you use hay as bedding or not, you will need a hayrack to keep the feeding hay dry and clean.

Ensure your hutch is well-guarded against foxes, badgers and other predators. These animals can open latches, so add a padlock or put on a bolt. If you are making your own hutch, do not use chicken wire – it can be chewed through. Runs should be too heavy for a fox to tip over. Wire pegs will help to pin the frame to the ground. Make sure the run has a roof or wire lid – birds of prey can also attack pet rabbits. Check that your rabbit can't dig out of his run and that no carnivores can dig in to get it. Paving stones, or wire sunk under the turf is the solution.

In winter, wrap the water bottle with bubble wrap to keep it warm and change frequently if it freezes. A pet warmer, carefully wrapped, can help keep the sleeping quarters from becoming too cold. Rabbits can freeze to death.

If you have more than one rabbit, make sure there is enough of everything, including food bowls. Every good rabbit must have its own bowl; otherwise they will fight to get a place at the trough. A builder's earthenware pipe can make a good place for moments when a bunny wants her privacy.

Carrot Cuisine

Clean water, fresh daily, is a must for all rabbits. A water bottle attached to the front of the hutch may be less messy than an earthenware bowl. Check that it doesn't get blocked with ice in winter or go green in summer. Some bunnies prefer bowls.

Three quarters of your bunny's diet should be good sweet hay. Buy good-quality hay or kiln-dried grass – not alfalfa, which is too rich. The longer each hay stem, the

better is it for the rabbit. And the
harder the rabbit has to chew her
hay, the less she will get tooth
trouble. Store the hay in a dry
place. Damp, mouldy or dusty hay
is the last straw for a rabbit.

Pellets are better than mixes. Choose the pellet with the highest amount of fibre. Feed these once a day in the morning and if your rabbit hasn't eaten every scrap by noon, feed less the following day. The bunnies have got to have room for their hay. If you must feed a mix, don't refill the bowl until the rabbit has eaten almost every bit of it – to stop your bunny just picking out the rich bits.

Beware of rabbit food sold loose from open bins or sacks. Loose pet food can contain invisible moulds. Some of the packaged hay sold in shops is poor quality, so choose a reputable brand.

Clean grass is the best fresh food for rabbits – the coarser the better, but never feed lawn clippings. You can also feed chickweed, clover, dandelions, groundsel, knapweed, plantain, shepherd's purse, sow thistle, vetch and even brambles. Nettles, cut before flowering, and dried make good hay. Feed dandelions in moderation.

As well as grass, garden vegetables can include carrot tops, celery, and parsley. Pea pods,

kale, Brussels sprouts, spinach, sweet corn, watercress and spring greens are fine in moderate quantities. Feed only small amounts of root vegetables like Swedes or carrots. Carrots are for rabbits what chocolates are to kids.

F ruit should only be given as a special treat – not more than one tablespoonful a day for a 4lb (2 kg) rabbit. Tiny fragments of apples, bananas, pears, peaches, strawberries and melon make good treats if used sparingly.

D on't feed your bunny alcohol, salty foods, or chocolate. Some human foods can poison a rabbit and most human foods are far too rich. You don't eat rabbit pellets. Why should your rabbit eat pizza?

Do not feed lettuce, beetroot tops, raw beans, potato, rhubarb, or avocado. And don't give your bunny the seeds or stones in fruit. Some garden plants like foxgloves, horsetails, monkshood, yew, and any plant growing from a bulb can also be poisonous.

Branches of apple trees, hazel and willow are the equivalent of a bone for a dog! Some rabbits are one-bunny destruction units, especially unspayed female bunnies. If you don't give them things to chew they will try to chew their hutch, the side of the run, your shoes, your new sweater, your

favourite book, electric cables, table legs, skirting board or books. Don't underestimate bunny chew-chew power.

Never feed sticky treats. You can love a bunny to death if he gets too fat. Look for the hay-based and fibre-rich treats now available. Better still, use wild plants like clover and dandelion as treats. Or tiny bits of carrots or apple. Locust beans, which are still sold in pet shops, are dangerous to rabbits.

If you decide to change your rabbit's diet, do it slowly over a month, mixing the new food in with the old and slowly increasing the proportion of the new.

Put your bunny on a diet if she is too fat. Familiar signs in humans as well as rabbits include hanging dewlaps or double chins,

saggy tummies and (in rabbits only!) dirty bottoms. You cannot feel her ribs for fat. Regular weigh-ins will reveal if either of you are putting on too much weight. Slim together! There are now diet foods for bunnies too, but there is no substitute for exercise.

If your bunny stops eating, or stops eating hard food like carrots, get help fast. Lack of appetite and no droppings are a veterinary emergency.

How Clean is Your Hutch?

Check your bunny's hutch daily and do a quick clean. Clean thoroughly twice weekly, removing and replacing all the bedding. In hot weather be extra thorough. Use a pet-safe disinfectant if you need one. Disinfectants that turn cloudy when diluted are poisonous to animals.

Outside bunnies can be litter-trained too. Never use clay or clumping litter, shavings from conifers like pine or cedar, or litter made from corncobs. Use litter made out of straw, safe wood shavings or paper, or put down a thick wad of newspaper. Put lots of hay on top. Rabbits like to chew

while they poo. And when the rabbit is eating hay, she is less likely to chew the paper. You can clear the tray by rolling up the paper with the hay inside.

Clean the litter tray daily but do not make it too clean. It should be free of wet patches but still smell like a toilet. Do not use strong-smelling deodorants; the smell will push bunny off his tray and he might start going somewhere less suitable.

If you must change the type of litter, then change over a period of at least two months, slowly putting in the new litter about a handful at a time.

Some litter-trained rabbits will leave their droppings outside

the tray to mark their territory with 'Bunny was here'. Neutering helps reduce this.

Special moist shiny droppings are eaten by your bunny. This may seem disgusting to humans, but it is nature's way of recycling the fibre a rabbit needs. If these moist droppings are left in the hutch or get stuck to the bunny's bottom, there is risk of fatal fly strike.

Home-Sweet-Home Bunny

A house is not a home without a house bunny. Be bunny-proud instead of house-proud. Lighten up your living room with a pair of bright eyes, four scampering paws and a delightfully twitching nose.

House rabbits need their home within the house: a place where they can retreat when life gets too much – and a place where they can be shut away at times for

safety's sake. An indoor dog-crate is often the best solution and it's useful for taking your house bunny on visits to relatives.

Because your rabbit's home is inside a warm house, it can be lined with pure wool, carpet off-cut or fleece instead of barley straw. Plastic dog or cat beds are also useful.

Rabbits can be house trained. Use a large cat-litter tray or a special corner tray. Take some soiled material and place it in a litter tray. Place the tray over the area that the rabbit is already using as a toilet.

A litter tray must be in a secluded location. If your rabbit has several rooms for his territory, put a litter tray in each one. Bunnies are barmy about ensuite arrangements.

Junk mail and bills will no longer trouble you. When you come home from work you may find your house bunny has shredded the lot. Buy a mailbox if you want to keep those letters out of reach.

They also enjoy destroying books,
so keep these out of reach if you
want to read them.

A baby gate, or puppy-pen panel,
with extra chicken wire if
needed, will stop your bunny going
upstairs and sleeping on your bed.

A very large rabbit can squeeze into a tiny space more suitable for a mouse. With uncanny skill they will choose an area almost impossible for a human to reach. So block off the gaps behind the

refrigerator, underneath the oven, or at the back of the waste pipe belonging to the kitchen sink. Or get ready to lie on your back and wriggle to one side while trying to poke out the rabbit with a bamboo pole.

House rabbits will change your ideas of interior design. Shorten all floor-length curtains unless you want them fringed or frilled. Redecorate with paint not wallpaper. Use cling film, covered with cloth, to protect table legs. Bunny-proof your skirting boards using perspex panels from DIY shops. Wrap phone, computer and electric wires in tubing. You can use conduit or plastic wire tubing from hardware shops or fish-tank tubing from aquatic centres.

Moulded plugs make covering the wire difficult because you can't remove the plug and thread the wiring through. Split the tubing lengthways instead and close it up with tape. Don't risk your rabbit becoming a current bunny!

Rabbits love hanging about at the back of the sofa, and while they are there they find it fun to nibble. Place a large roll of cardboard behind the sofa for them to shelter in. Or make one with a roll of off-cut woollen carpet with the carpet side inwards. This keeps teeth marks off the loose covers.

Your cat or your dog may seem to love your house rabbit and be happy to play! But never leave them alone with a bunny. The sight of one lolloping by may prove too much for their self-control. For them, a running bunny is a meal on wheels. Sometimes it's the rabbit you can't trust. A particularly up-front bunny may attack a dog or cat!

Keep your house rabbit safe. Close the lavatory lid, the windows, doors . . . and turn off electrical appliances. You don't want a bun in the oven.

Enjoy vacuuming up the droppings and don't forget to wear your slippers first thing in the morning. Rabbit poo between your bare toes is not a good way to start the day!

Be wary of bunches of cut flowers or houseplants! Poinsettia, lilies and some other plants are poisonous. All of them will be nibbled, some will be upset, and your rabbit may try to dig his way into the pot. At least you have an excuse for getting rid of that unwanted pot-plant present!

Fence off the Christmas tree, or keep bunny out of the living room while it is there. Pine needles can hurt tender paws or get stuck in the gullet, so sweep them all up. Tree baubles can be dangerous if chewed or broken.

Fun for Bun

Bunnies move earth like bull-dozers. They dig. A child's plastic sandpit filled with half-sand half-peat will give your rabbit the chance to dig, without it undermining the whole lawn. Or make a digging box with straw and hay inside and a hole half-way up the side. A bunny's sandpit or digging box should be wide enough for her to turn round and deep enough for her to dig down her own height.

Bunnies like to burrow into dark places. Use cardboard rolls, earthenware pipes, or special pet tunnels to give them their own little warren. Or arrange several cardboard boxes with entrance holes to make an above-ground burrow.

Toys make a funny bunny. Stuff a kitchen-roll tube with straw or hay. Household cardboard refuse like cereal boxes, paper-hanky boxes, or almost anything in cardboard or paper can become a bunny toy. Paper (not plastic) bags are good fun too. Keep an eye out for old straw hats and willow baskets at boot sales. Avoid plastic

toys or toys made of sweetcorn kernels. These are dangerous to rabbits.

Bunnies rarely retrieve but they like tossing things about. Toilet-roll tubes, dried pine-cones, used sticky-tape rolls or light cat-toys will be picked up and thrown about. Some bunnies will enjoy nudging a football about the run. House bunnies particularly enjoy noisy toys in the small hours of the morning!

Make a play centre by cutting an entrance hole into a wooden box to place in the outside run. Or use a cardboard box for indoors. Put wood shavings and hay inside. You can even buy your bunny a special cardboard playhouse.

King of the castle and mountaineering are good bunny games, so give your rabbit things to sit on – upturned storage boxes, garden stools and such-like. Put a wooden plank over two bricks with one side touching to make a corner. Add a second layer of bricks. Your bunny can sit on top or underneath this. If you have a house rabbit, he will use the sofa for mountaineering games.

Instead of putting food in a bowl, hide it so your rabbit has to forage for it. Or feed it in a puzzle toy, such as a treat ball with holes for the pellets to come out. Most rabbits enjoy working to get their food.

Teach your young and healthy rabbit show-jumping, as they do in Scandinavia. At four or five months, a rabbit can be taught to jump over miniature fences. You will need kindness, patience, a special harness and lots of healthy rabbit-treats. Children should always have adult supervision for this. Check with your vet that your rabbit is fit enough before starting. This vigorous exercise is not suitable for elderly rabbits or rabbits that have lived in hutches all their lives.

Sex, Love and Friendship – Bunny Style

If your bunny starts running around you in circles and spraying jets of urine at you, he hasn't had the snip. This behaviour is a sign he fancies you – it is rabbit courtship. Be grateful that human males give chocolates!

If you are male and your bunny is male, those jets of urine may not

be courtship after all. Some male
rabbits spray on other males they
consider inferior. Therapy may
help you come to terms with this,
but don't forget the snip (for him).

The buck stops here. Neuter your male bunny. He will be happier and better-tempered after the snip and you won't have the patter of too many tiny paws.

Rabbits breed like . . . well, rabbits! Spay your does. This will spare them repeated pregnancies, false pregnancies, or the risk of cancer. Besides, unspayed female rabbits have the urge to dig nests – in your sofa, in the lawn and in the corner of the hutch.

A hot cross bunny can hurt if he attacks your ankles or hands. Neutering prevents aggression between rabbits and humans and between rabbit and rabbit.

Don't just place a new rabbit into your bunny's home. She will think it is an intruder and attack him. Keep them side by side for several weeks where they can see and smell each other. Then introduce them on neutral ground – in the spare bedroom, the bathroom,

even in the back of a car. Better still
get your new rabbit from a good
rescue shelter that will do this for
you.

Make sure there is plenty of
room in their new living
quarters, more than one water
bottle, several places of refuge like
sleeping quarters or large earthenware tunnels, and as many food
bowls as rabbits. Hoppiness is not
having to queue.

Rabbits identify friend and foe
by smell as well as looks. If one
bunny has been to the vet, he may

smell wrong to his companion and
most animals hate the smell of a
vet. So take both the sick bunny and
his healthy companion to the vet's
surgery.

If a fight breaks out, separate the rabbits immediately to restore warren peace. A little squabble is normal from time to time, but a real fight means fur flying or even spilt blood. Then reintroduce them gradually over several days on neutral ground. Call in a bunny shrink for help with this.

Keep small (human) girls under constant supervision. Small girls like dressing up animals and picking up bunnies for a cuddle. They don't try to pick up the family dog, so why should they do this to a rabbit?

Do not loom over your rabbit. It scares him. Approach him at his own level. Never, ever, pick up a rabbit by his ears. Instead place one hand under your rabbit's bottom to take his weight, and the other between or just behind his forelegs.

When one of your rabbits dies, let her companion see the body. It's kinder to let her know what has happened. Later you can

find her a new friend with the help
of a rescue shelter.

Does and Don'ts

Don't let a bunny problem become a rabbit habit. Rabbits don't grow out of behaviour problems. They grow into them. Get early help from a bunny shrink.

Never punish. It doesn't work. Instead reward good behaviour and ignore bad behaviour. House rabbits often develop little ways to get your attention, ranging from looking winsome to biting your ankle. A house bunny is very good at training his humans. If you

shout at him, he knows he has got your attention so just ignore him. Give attention when he is behaving well.

Bunnies that bite are frightened, not vicious. They may not have been handled when they were young, with the result that they are terrified of being picked up and held high in the air. Sometimes they kick out and become a Thugs Bunny. Wear thick gloves if you need to handle a biter, or better still use a travel box as a taxi. Use this to carry them from their hutch to their run.

If your rabbit scratches, nips or kicks when you put your hand in her house, back off. She's just defending her burrow. Sometimes it helps to rub your hands in her bedding so that you smell like her. Shut her in her sleeping quarters while you clean the living area of her house, and vice versa when you clean the sleeping area. Or clean up while she is in her run.

Sometimes food becomes an issue. Some rabbits defend their food bowl and become hopping mad when you want to take it. Change where you put the bowl, so it's not always in one place. Offer him something nice to munch before you take out the bowl to refill it.

Tame a frightened bunny by sitting on the floor and reading a book. Rabbits are inquisitive creatures and he will eventually come to investigate you. Food treats help too!

A Long and Hoppy Life

Choose a vet carefully. You want a bunny-lover who knows about proper feeding, teeth care and neutering.

Make your new vet happy too by getting proper bunny insurance.

Train your bunny to enter her travel box by putting a piece of delicious food inside it whenever you want her to enter it. At other times leave the box with some food inside where the rabbit will come across it. A travel box left in their usual run makes travelling less stressful because they are in a familiar place.

Vaccinate against myxomatosis and viral haemorrhagic disease (VHD). These are killer diseases.

Get teeth checked at vaccination time and whenever bunny is at the vet's surgery. Ask your vet to teach you how to check teeth between visits. Rabbit incisors grow continuously – about a centimetre a month. This causes dental trouble if they don't have enough hay and other things to chew. Some breeds seem particularly prone to tooth trouble and you may need to check frequently.

Toothache makes humans and bunnies miserable and cross. Symptoms are wet chin, wet paws, difficulty eating, matted or dirty fur, runny eyes, loss of appetite, lumps along the jaw line or a dirty bottom. A rabbit with toothache may hate being touched near the head or may sit hunched up and apathetic with pain.

Fur's fur. If you groom your bunny regularly, there will be a little less fur on your clothes. Groom long-haired bunnies daily with a wide-toothed human comb, then a finer-toothed one. Under the chin, inside the front legs, and around the bottom are particularly likely to mat up so do them carefully. Or clip the coat completely every four to six weeks.

Check your rabbit's bottom daily in summer. A dirty bottom means flies may lay their

eggs and their maggots could eat your rabbit alive. In summer use *Rearguard*. Insect deterrents and fly screens are not enough.

A sticky bottom is a sign that something is wrong. Rabbits do special droppings that are moist and shiny. They eat these, as they come out of their backsides. If they are not eating them, the cause may be too rich a diet, too fat a bunny, tooth trouble or arthritis. Get your vet's advice immediately and change the diet to include much more hay.

Fleas and mites. Never use sprays or potions without asking a vet if they are safe. Some preparations are safe for cats or dogs but kill rabbits.

Learn to recognise a bunny in pain. It's not easy. They don't whimper or scream. They sit hunched up, eyes half-closed, and sometimes grind their teeth. A previously gentle rabbit may bite. There may be changes in the latrine area or litter tray, diarrhoea or loss of appetite. Continued pain may lead to fur-pulling or self-mutilation. If in the slightest doubt, get veterinary advice immediately.

Let your bunny go when it is time to say goodbye. If there's a heaven for animals, he will hop into it easily. A painless death is your last gift to him.

Useful Information

More information on rabbits, including sticky bottom and fly strike, can be found on my website: www.celiahaddon.co.uk

THE RABBIT WELFARE ASSOCIATION

P.O. Box 603, Horsham, West Sussex RH13 5WL. Helpline: 0890 046 5249. http://www.rabbit welfare.co.uk

The place to start for all rabbit information. RWA can give advice, help find rabbit rescue shelters, rabbit friendly vets, and boarding establishments.

RABBIT BEHAVIOUR ADVISORY GROUP

www.rabbitbehaviour.co.uk. For a fee, three qualified rabbit behaviourists will deal with rabbit behaviour problems.

RABBIT TOYS

Try the shop at the RWA (see above). Willow balls, tunnels, teepees, feeders, good hay and other chew toys are available from West Wales Willows 01437 741714

or www.westwaleswillows.co.uk.
Play castles and other toys from
Bunny Mail www.bunnymail.co.uk
or 0151 428 9243. Pet warmers and
bunny warren tunnel from www.
snugglesafe.co.uk or 01903 730811.

RABBIT OUTDOOR HOUSING

The following firms stock large
hutches (ignore their smaller ones):
Pet House www.pethouse-uk.com,
01245 401009; Forsham Cottage
Arks www.forshamcottagearks.com,
01233 820229 (remembering that a
rabbit can't reach the lowest area of
the ark); SPR Centre www.spr
centre.co.uk, 01243 542815.

RABBIT INDOOR HOUSING

Try a dog crate or make your own enclosure using puppy panels. There should be room for food, water, litter tray as well as bedding. Try www.shawspet.co.uk, 01296 429333, or www.croftonline.co.uk, 01257 484200. If big enough crates are not in stock, good pet shops will order them.

INSURANCE

Pet Plan offers a covered-for-life guarantee. Contact: 0845 0771934 or www.petplan.co.uk

Acknowledgement

The sentence, 'A rabbit is for life not for Easter', is used by permission of Dogs Trust.

Thanks to Dogs Trust, hundreds of abandoned dogs are re-homed and looked after for life. Dogs Trust is opposed to the destruction of any healthy dog and is working towards the day when all dogs can enjoy a happy life free from the threat of unnecessary destruction. If you would like to know more about Dogs Trust and its work visit www.dogstrust.org.uk